SCHIRMER'S LIBRARY
OF MUSICAL CLASSICS

Vol. 905

J. B. ACCOLAŸ

Concerto No. 1

In A minor

For the Violin

With Piano Accompaniment

Edited and Fingered by

OTTO K. SCHILL

✣

G. SCHIRMER, Inc.

DISTRIBUTED BY

HAL•LEONARD®
CORPORATION

7777 W. BLUEMOUND RD. P.O. BOX 13819 MILWAUKEE, WI 53213

Revised and edited by
Otto K. Schill

Concerto

J. B. Accolay

Piano

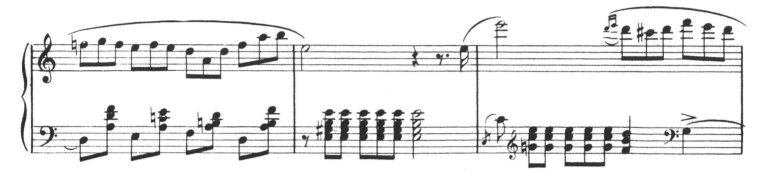

19105

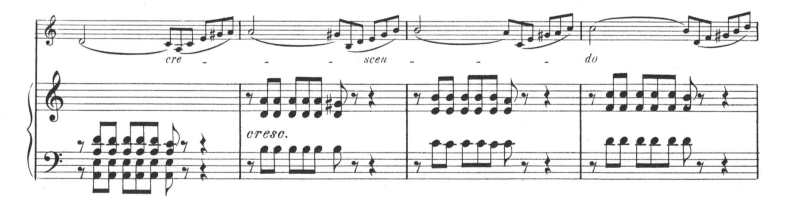

19105

Violin

Violin

SCHIRMER'S LIBRARY
OF MUSICAL CLASSICS

Vol. 905

J. B. ACCOLAŸ

Concerto No. I
In A minor

For the Violin

With Piano Accompaniment

Edited and Fingered by

OTTO K. SCHILL

⊕

G. SCHIRMER, Inc.

DISTRIBUTED BY

HAL•LEONARD®
CORPORATION

7777 W. BLUEMOUND RD. P.O. BOX 13019 MILWAUKEE, WI 53213

Concerto

Revised and edited by
Otto K. Schill

Violin

J. B. Accolay

Allegro moderato

largamente e ritenuto

Maggiore